Presents

A Decodable Play-Based, Reading Primer

High Frequency Words and Short Vowel Sounds

(Consonant Vowel Consonant Words and Vowel Consonant Words)

Caroline Wilcox Ugurlu, PhD

Letters Are Characters ®
presents
Letters are Builders
A Play-Based, Reading Primer
1st Edition
All Rights Reserved.
Copyright © 2024 Caroline Wilcox Ugurlu, Ph.D.

The opinions expressed in this manuscript are solely the opinions of the author and do not represent the opinions or thoughts of the publisher. The author has represented and warranted full ownership and/or legal right to publish all the materials in this book.

This book may not be reproduced, transmitted, or stored in whole or in part by any means, including graphic, electronic, or mechanical without the express written consent of the publisher except in the case of brief quotations embodied in critical articles and reviews.

Outskirts Press, Inc.
http://www.outskirtspress.com

ISBN: 978-1-9772-7142-6

Illustrations by Caroline Wilcox Ugurlu, Ph.D.

Author Photo © 2024 Terry Augustyn, Nutmeg Photography. All rights reserved – used with permission.

This book has been designed using assets from Freepik.com

Outskirts Press and the "OP" logo are trademarks belonging to Outskirts Press, Inc.

PRINTED IN THE UNITED STATES OF AMERICA

Dedication

For Dana

And for Jayne Bentzen who works to ensure that kids learn to read.
And for all kids learning to read - know that if it is hard for you to learn to read,
it has nothing to do with how smart you are or how special and beautiful your brain is.

When learning to read
our brains make connections at differing speeds.

Take the time that your child needs
for you're planting seeds.

Seeds that flower into the ability to read
and will help children to succeed.

Some kids may need lots of repetitive purposeful play
to wire their brains, they are made that way.

This does not relate to being smart
keep this message in your heart.

Learning should not cause suffering.
If it does, a child needs buffering.

Your knowledge of this is transformative.
Learning the science of reading is critically informative.

Enjoy your time together as your child learns to read.
These days are precious and they pass with great speed.

Love of learning is freedom and power
and you can build it like a fortress with a tower.

Level by level up to the top
when a child loves to read, learning will never stop.

So learn together holding hands, heart to heart.
You are giving your child a prodigious start.

Table of Contents

Consonant Review 2-3

Digraph Review 4-5

Letter A Review 6-7
The Sad Cat 8-19

Letter E Review 20-21
Ben met Jen the Hen 22-33

Letter I Review 34-35
Jim the Fit Pig 36-47

Letter O Review 48-49
Mom Frog 50-61

Letter U Review 62-63
Bud the Mutt 64-75

Letter Y Review 76-77
Ty and Sky Fly - Single Syllable words ending in y 78-89

Vowel Review 90-91

The Cat is Not Sad Now 92-103

High Frequency Words 104-139

Introduction

All children benefit from explicit, repetitive, multisensory, play-based reading instruction. Some children need more repetition when learning to read than others. This is independent of intelligence.

When children are at play, they are relaxed and best able to learn. All young mammals play, it is essential and purposeful. So, Letters are Characters® books and other materials are designed to be seriously playful.

When using this book, tell your little learner that the words that are not in the Letters are Characters® font are high frequency words. These words are memorized like pictures or logos. These are the only words that emerging readers don't decode or sound out. You will find them at the back of the book. Practice them. They make up 50-75% of early readers. Recognizing them helps learners to conserve cognitive fuel so that they can focus on meaningful learning efficiently.

In this Letters are Builders decodable book, learners will be mastering short vowel sounds and applying the general rule that vowel consonant words (at, et, it, ot, ut) and vowel consonant words (bat, bet, bit, bot and but) require vowels to "say" their short sound. They will also learn that y says the long i sound at the end of one syllable words that end in y (by, my).

Have them use their fingers to tap each sound and blend them.

You are working on fluency/automaticity which means that words can be read without decoding because they are familiar. That is why sentences repeat. The new sentence is highlighted. You will notice that illustrations are on pages that follow the decodable text and that there is a space for your child to draw their own illustrations. This is because pictures should only be used to confirm that the words have been read correctly. Sometimes pictures on the page can lead to guessing, and that makes it seem like children are reading when, in fact, they are not. More than 87% of English words follow the rules and reading is best taught through explicit learning of the rule followed by applying it until it is mastered.

Encourage your learner to touch the text. It helps when they get stuck on a word. Have them use their fingers to tap each sound and then blend them.

When a child is working through the process, try to avoid rushing them or saying "no." Saying "try again" is best because it maintains the learning flow. Kids can't learn optimally if they feel anxious.

When kids learn to read they are creating neural pathways in their brains! These pathways are built with each repetitive, play-based fun session.

Love the singular moments that you will share.

Now dear reader let's begin.

Consonant Review

If your child needs consonant review, use this page. The sound can be practiced by saying the first sound in the letter's favorite food and personality trait. Vowels are the most difficult for most children so the focus of this primer is working through one vowel sound at a time until mastery is achieved.

Personality trait: Bouncy
Favorite food: Bananas

Personality trait: Happy
Favorite food: Hamburgers

Personality trait: Caring
Favorite food: Celery and Carrots

Personality trait: Jumpy
Favorite food: Jawbreakers

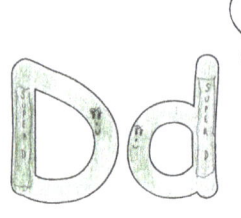 

Personality trait: Dazzling and dandy
Favorite food: Doughnuts

Personality trait: Kooky and kicky
Favorite food: Kebabs

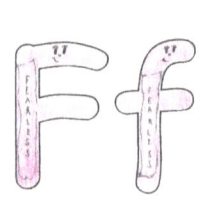 

Personality trait: Fabulous
Favorite food: French fries

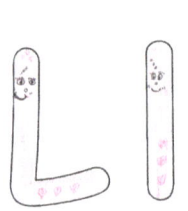 

Personality trait: Loving
Favorite food: Lollipops

Personality trait: Generous & giving
Favorite food: Grapes

Personality trait: Munchy
Favorite food: Marshmallows and almost anything that will fit in M's mouth.

Personality trait: Negative
Favorite food: Nothing. She doesn't like anything! She'll eat nasty nuggets if she is hungry.

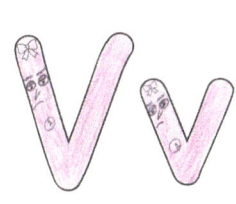 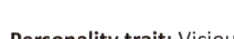

Personality trait: Vicious
Favorite food: Victorious veggies (Only blue-ribbon prize winners will do!)

Personality trait: Pee-ceful!
Favorite food: They like their food pureed in a liquid form. Peas, pineapple, and fruit punch are favorites.

Personality trait: Wonderful and wobbly
Favorite food: Watermelon and wiggly worms

Personality trait: Quizzical
Favorite food: Quiche (real Q's eat quiche) and quince fruit. Have you ever tried it?

Personality trait: Extraordinarily greedy. She chops her food with a tiny ax. (ks sound of x)
Favorite food: Not hungry. She is too busy looking for extra gold. She does like cookies shaped like an X.

Personality trait: Ready and raring to go
Favorite food: Radishes. Wait, those are for her rabbit. Raspberries.

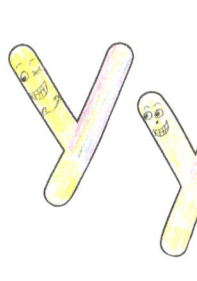 

Personality trait: He is a yes-man and can sound like long e or long i!
Favorite food: Yellow squash and my candy

Personality trait: Smiley and loves smelling roses (z sound of s)
Favorite food: Slushies with strawberries

Personality trait: Zippy and full of zest for life
Favorite food: Ziti made with zucchini!

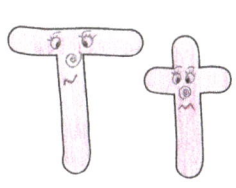 

Personality trait: Tip-Top
Favorite food: Tater Tots with Tea

Digraph Review

Digraphs are two letters that come together to make one sound.

ck is a digraph - two letters that come together to make one sound. Think of them hugging and the hug changes the sounds that they make!

C and K come together and say /k/ and they can only sit at the end of a **one syllable** word as in sock or clock!

Do they get along? ☐ Yes ☒ No!

K does not want to cuddle c! He shouts so you only hear his sound! K says YUCK when c tries to cuddle!

What snacks do they like to eat when they are together? All snack packs and especially crackers and pepperjack cheese.

ch is a digraph - two letters that come together to make one sound. Think of them hugging and the hug changes the sounds that they make!

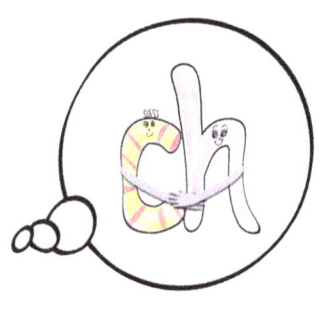

C and h come together and say ch as in choo, choo or /k/ as in chorus!

Do they get along? ☒ Yes ☐ No

What snacks do they like to eat when they are together? Chips!

4

sh is a digraph - two letters that come together to make one sound.
Think of them hugging and the hug changes the sounds that they make!

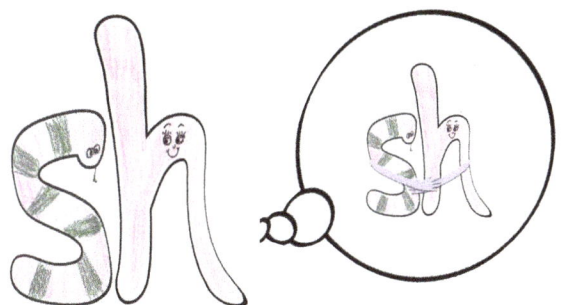

s and h come together and say /sh/ as in ship shape!

Do they get along? ☑ Yes ☐ No
Yes, they both share!

What food do they like to eat when they are together? Sherbet and shortcake!

wh is a digraph - two letters that come together to make one sound.
Think of them hugging and the hug changes the sounds that they make!

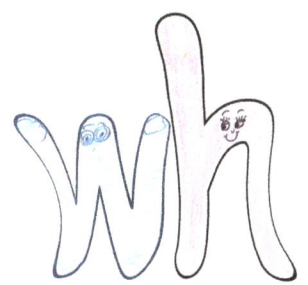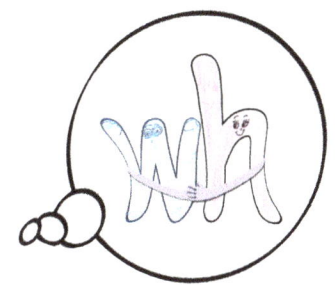

w and h come together and say /w/ or /hw? as in whiskers!

Do they get along? ☑ Yes ☐ No
Yes, w and h like to do a happy wiggle dance!

What food do they like to eat when they are together? Wheat toast!

ph is a digraph - two letters that come together to make one sound.
Think of them hugging and the hug changes the sounds that they make!

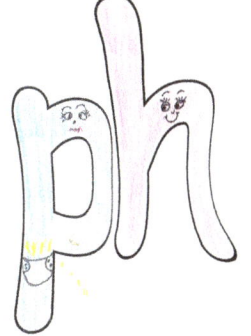

p and h come together and say /f/ as in phone or phonics!

Do they get along? ☑ Yes ☐ No
Yes, they both say "take our photo we are friends!"

What food do they like to eat when they are together? Pho!

LETTER "A" REVIEW

A is a vowel. He is a two-sound guy.

Pronounce the short vowel (ă sound) when you see a lowercase letter and the long vowel (ā sound) when you see a capital letter.

Daddy A likes to be first.
When he can't be, his mood is the worst!
He says (insert short vowel sound ă as in apple and ā, which is his name).
"When I am not first, I am a-a-aggravated! I need to be the leader! When the word starts with a-a-a like *at*, it is great. But not when it is b-a-t or c-a-t, bat the *b* and cut that *c*. Let me a-a-at 'em. I am the leader, the number one letter in the a-a-alphabet, and when I am a-a-angry, I act like a mad Ape."

And when the letters don't move out of the w-a-y, A uses his long sound to boss people around. (Insert the long sound of A here.) A, A, A, A, A, get out of the wAy. Move W, A!

His little son, baby a, looks on and says, "A, a, a. D-a-d, Dad, I am going to grow up to be just like you!"

Personality trait: Aggravated
Favorite food: Apple

A is a vowel. Vowels are the letters that stick words together.

Trace me with your finger!
Draw me in the air.
Make me with clay.

All vowels are multicolored because they do lots of jobs and make more than one sound.

I am a sad cat.

Kid, tap and blend the letters that are characters and read the words that are in black (high frequency words) without tapping and blending. Never use pictures to "read." Look at the pictures on the next page ONLY to confirm that you understood the words. I get so mad when you don't use us to read the words <u>WE</u> letters build.

I am a sad cat.

I sat on Pat the rat.

Close your eyes and make a picture in your mind with the words you just read. Turn the page and see what the author/illustrator imagined. Do they match what you thought the words said? Draw your own interpretation below the picture on the page. Everyone's pictures are a little different. That is part of the magic of reading.

I am a sad cat.

Can you find the tiny vowels (a) in the illustration? Draw your illustration in the box below.

I sat on Pat the rat.

Can you find the tiny vowels (a) in the illustration? Draw your illustration in the box below.

I am a sad cat.

I sat on Pat the rat.

And, Pat the rat is mad.

I am a sad cat.

I sat on Pat the rat.

And, Pat the rat is mad.

Pat the rat had a bat.

And, Pat the rat is mad.

Can you find the tiny vowels (a) in the illustration? Draw your illustration in the box below.

Pat the rat had a bat.

Can you find the tiny vowels (a) in the illustration? Draw your illustration in the box below.

I am a sad cat.

I sat on Pat the rat.

And, Pat the rat is mad.

Pat the rat had a bat.

I ran.

I am a sad cat.
I sat on Pat the rat.
And, Pat the rat is mad.
Pat the rat had a bat.
I ran.
The bat was mad at me too!

I ran.

Can you find the tiny vowels (a) in the illustration? Draw your illustration in the box below.

The bat was mad at me too!

Can you find the tiny vowels (a) in the illustration? Draw your illustration in the box below.

LETTER "E" REVIEW

E is a vowel. He is a two-sound guy.

Daddy E is scared every day. But he can be the bravest for all of his friends, quietly empowering them.

He says (insert short vowel sound ĕ as in elephant and ē, which is his name). He says, "Eeeeeee," as if he has seen a ghost and "e-e-e" to empower himself. " I get so scared when you don't use us letters to read words, WE letters build."

Little baby e looks on and beams at his dad. He is e-e-encouraging and E-E-Eager to please, just like his dad.

Personality trait: Eager and empathetic
Favorite food: Eggplant

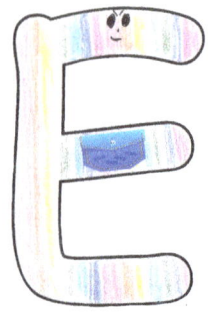 

For consonant-vowel-consonant e words, brave E and e store macrons in their pockets so that they can give them to vowel friends when they need them!

E is a vowel. Vowels are the letters that stick words together.

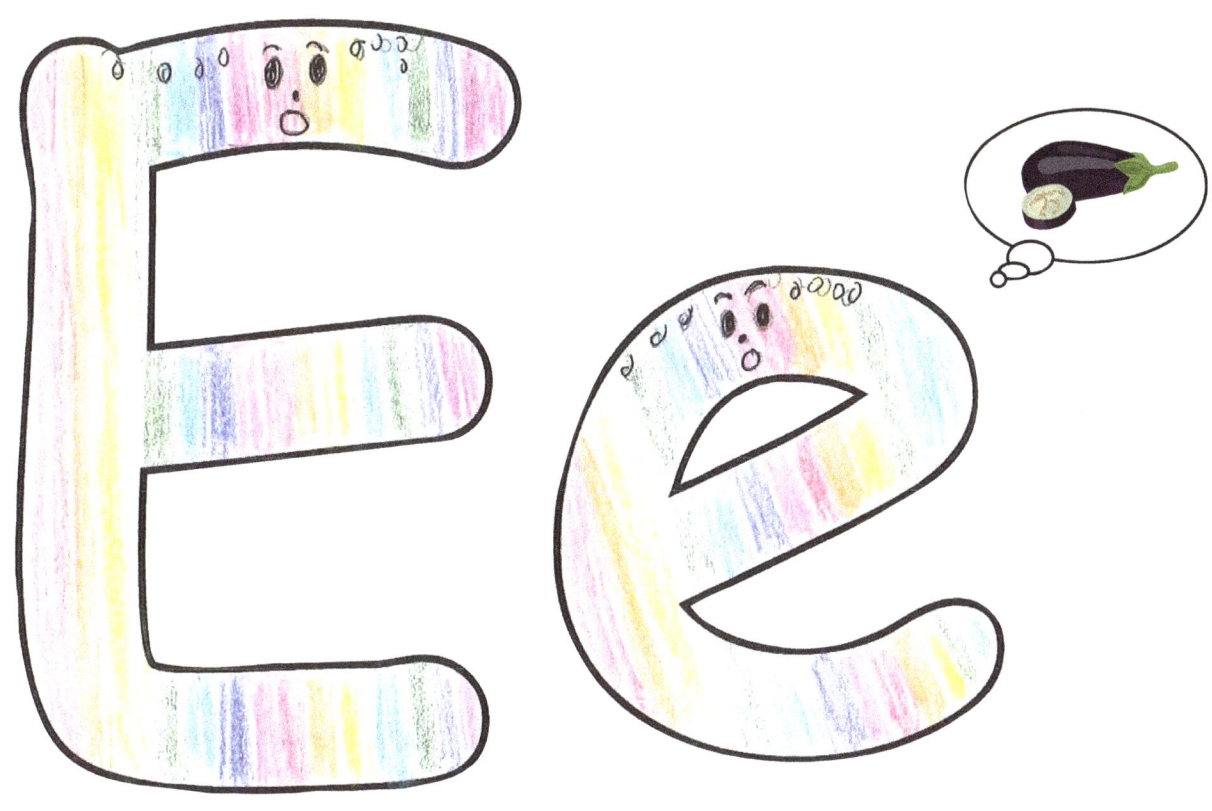

All vowels are multicolored because they do lots of jobs and make more than one sound.

 E can be brave too! When he sits at the end of words, he helps vowels say their long sounds!

Ben met a hen.

Kid, tap and blend the letters that are characters and read the words that are in black (high frequency words) without tapping and blending. Never use pictures to "read." Look at the pictures on the next page ONLY to confirm that you understood the words. I get so scared when you don't use us to read the words <u>WE</u> letters build.

Ben met a hen.

Jen the hen is red.

Close your eyes and make a picture in your mind with the words you just read. Turn the page and see what the author/illustrator imagined. Do they match what you thought the words said? Draw your own interpretation below the picture on the page. Everyone's pictures are a little different. That is part of the magic of reading.

Ben met a hen.

Can you find the tiny vowels (e) in the illustration? Draw your illustration in the box below.

Jen the hen is red.

Can you find the tiny vowels (e) in the illustration? Draw your illustration in the box below.

Ben met a hen.

Jen the hen is red.

Jen pecks* Ben!

26 *In single syllable words, the digraph ck is used for the k sound at the end of words.

Ben met a hen.

Jen the hen is red.

Jen pecks Ben!

Ben's neck is red.

Jen pecks Ben!

Can you find the tiny vowels (e) in the illustration? Draw your illustration in the box below.

Ben's neck is red.

Can you find the tiny vowels (e) in the illustration? Draw your illustration in the box below.

Ben met a hen.

Jen the hen is red.

Jen pecks Ben!

Ben's neck is red.

Ben went to the vet.

Ben met a hen.

Jen the hen is red.

Jen pecks Ben!

Ben's neck is red.

Ben went to the vet.

"Do not peck Ben," said the vet.

Ben went to the vet.

Can you find the tiny vowels (e) in the illustration? Draw your illustration in the box below.

"Do not peck Ben," said the vet.

Can you find the tiny vowels (e) in the illustration? Draw your illustration in the box below.

LETTER "I" REVIEW

I is a vowel. He is a two-sound guy.

Daddy I is so selfish. He just thinks about what he wants all day long and ignores everything else.

He says (insert short sound of ĭ) and (insert long sound of ī). "I don't care who wants what I-I-I want! I get bored when I need to listen i-i-intently to others because i-i-it is not i-i-interesting. I am interesting, and I want to sit with my i-i-iguana in an i-i-igloo, and eat i-i-ice cream now!"

His son, little baby i, blinks his dot at his dad and says, "I want more too, and I want to grow up and be i-i-interesting just like you!"

Personality trait: Interesting (to himself)
Favorite food: He has an itch for ice cream.

I is a vowel. Vowels are the letters that stick words together.

Trace me with your finger!
Draw me in the air.
Make me with clay.

All vowels are multicolored because they do lots of jobs and make more than one sound.

Jim is a pig.

Kid, tap and blend the letters that are characters and read the words that are in black (high frequency words) without tapping and blending. Never use pictures to "read." Look at the pictures on the next page ONLY to confirm that you understood the words. I get so irritated when you don't use us to read the words <u>WE</u> letters build.

Jim is a pig.

He is fit and did a jig.

Close your eyes and make a picture in your mind with the words you just read. Turn the page and see what the author/illustrator imagined. Do they match what you thought the words said? Draw your own interpretation below the picture on the page. Everyone's pictures are a little different. That is part of the magic of reading.

Jim is a pig.

Can you find the tiny vowels (i) in the illustration? Draw your illustration in the box below.

He is fit and did a jig.

Can you find the tiny vowels (i) in the illustration? Draw your illustration in the box below.

Jim is a pig.

He is fit and did a jig.

His wish is to win.

Jim is a pig.

He is fit and did a jig.

His wish is to win.

Sit Jim, your jig was a big hit.

His wish is to win.

Can you find the tiny vowels (i) in the illustration? Draw your illustration in the box below.

Sit Jim, your jig was a big hit.

Can you find the tiny vowels (i) in the illustration? Draw your illustration in the box below.

Jim is a pig.

He is fit and did a jig.

His wish is to win.

Sit Jim, your jig was a big hit.

You win, Jim.

Jim is a pig.

He is fit and did a jig.

His wish is to win.

Sit Jim, your jig was a big hit.

You win, Jim.

You win a fit, pig kit.

You win, Jim.

Can you find the tiny vowels (i) in the illustration? Draw your illustration in the box below.

You win a fit, pig kit.

Can you find the tiny vowels (i) in the illustration? Draw your illustration in the box below.

LETTER "O" REVIEW

O is a vowel. He is a two-sound guy.

Daddy O is as generous as they come. Giving gifts and getting gifts is his favorite thing.

He says (insert sounds here—ō as in Oh and ŏ as in ostrich). "Oh, Oh, Oh, you have a gift for me. Aw (short o sound), you shouldn't have! But I am so glad that you did! Oh, I have a gift for you too; aw (o), I hope you like it. It is a toy o-o-ostrich named o-o-ollie!"

His baby son o, the giver of the gift, rolls around and happily says oh and aw (o) as he watches his dad. "Oh, I want to be just like you, Daddy."

Personality trait: Open and optimistic

Favorite food: Oatmeal for breakfast and octopus on special occasions.

O is a vowel. Vowels are the letters that stick words together.

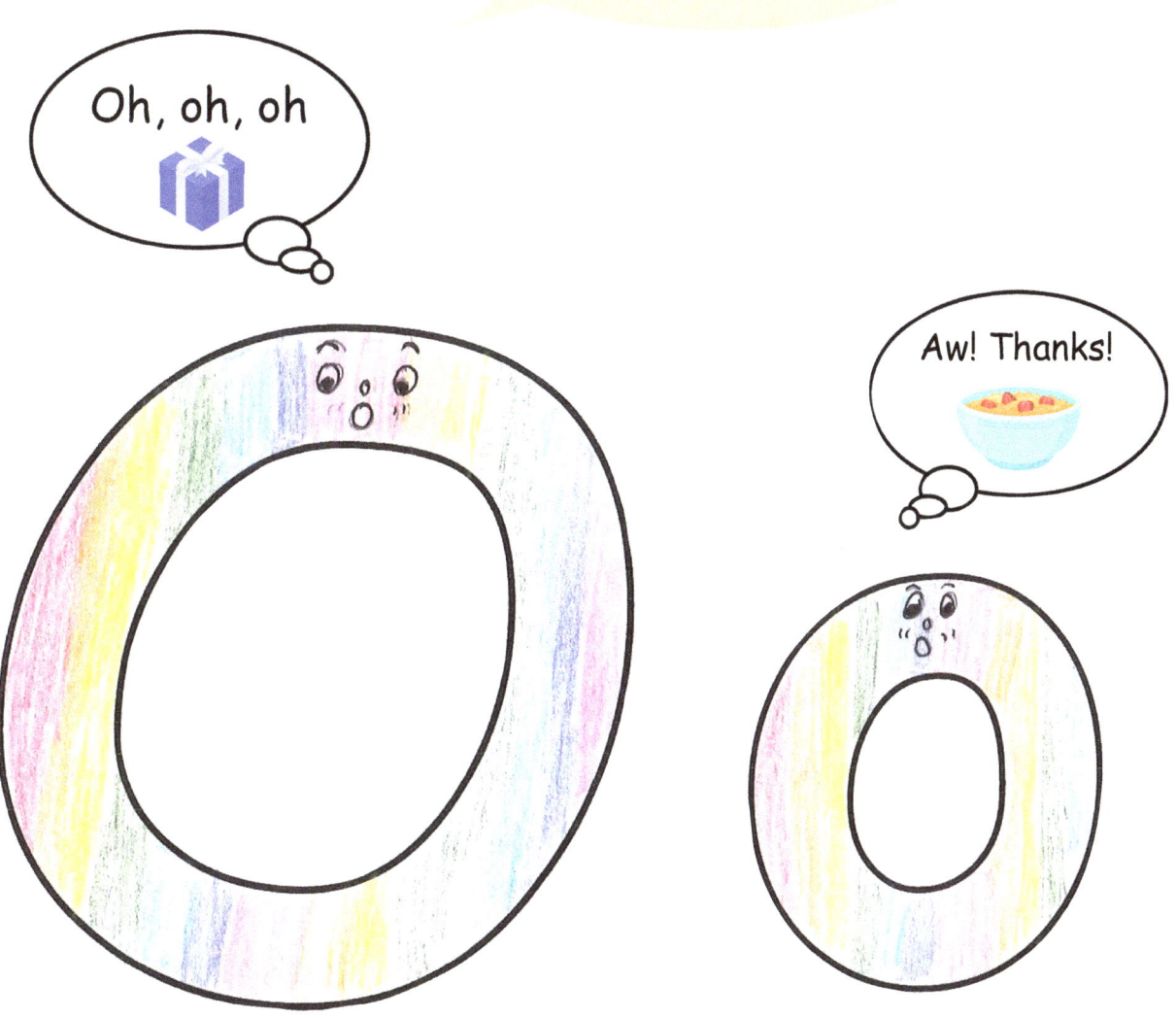

All vowels are multicolored because they do lots of jobs and make more than one sound.

Mom frog is the boss.*

Kid, tap and blend the letters that are characters and read the words that are in black (high frequency words) without tapping and blending. Never use pictures to "read." Look at the pictures on the next page ONLY to confirm that you understood the words. I get so surprised when you don't use us to read the words <u>WE</u> letters build.

*Single syllable words ending in f, l, s and sometimes z, have a double letter as in boss. These are the floss words.

Mom frog is the boss.

She hops in the bog.

Close your eyes and make a picture in your mind with the words you just read. Turn the page and see what the author/illustrator imagined. Do they match what you thought the words said? Draw your own interpretation below the picture on the page. Everyone's pictures are a little different. That is part of the magic of reading.

Mom frog is the boss.

Can you find the tiny vowels (o) in the illustration? Draw your illustration in the box below.

52

She hops in the bog.

Can you find the tiny vowels (o) in the illustration? Draw your illustration in the box below.

Mom frog is the boss.

She hops in the bog.

She hops, bobs and bops.

Mom frog is the boss.

She hops in the bog.

She hops, bobs and bops.

Frogs flop too.

She hops, bobs and bops.

Can you find the tiny vowels (o) in the illustration? Draw your illustration in the box below.

Frogs flop too.

Can you find the tiny vowels (o) in the illustration? Draw your illustration in the box below.

Mom frog is the boss.

She hops in the bog.

She hops, bobs and bops.

Frogs flop too.

Flop, hop, bob and bop mom frog!

Mom frog is the boss.

She hops in the bog.

She hops, bobs and bops.

Frogs flop too.

Flop, hop, bob and bop mom frog!

Mom frog and her son Bob hop and bop.

Flop, hop, bob and bop mom frog!

Can you find the tiny vowels (o) in the illustration? Draw your illustration in the box below.

Mom frog and her son Bob hop and bop.

Can you find the tiny vowels (o) in the illustration? Draw your illustration in the box below.

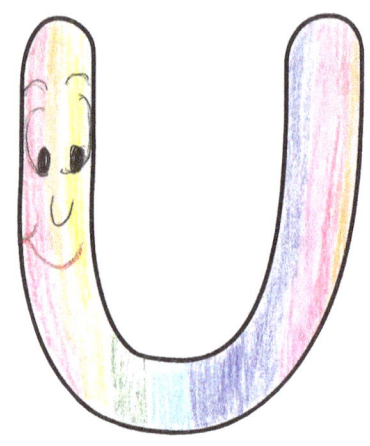

LETTER "U" REVIEW

U is a vowel. He is a two-sound guy.

U is u-u-utterly unselfish. He always wants to talk about you – U-U-U. He is a little shy and sometimes uses his short sound to get the conversation going. He is one of the nicest letters of all.

He says (insert two sounds here: ū (U) and ŭ (u) as in umbrella). "You are u-u-unique. I want to hear all about you. What do you like to eat, u-u-umbrella fruit? What do you like for dessert, u-u-upside-down cake? What is your favorite color? Tell me about you."

Little baby u always shares and always thinks of others too. "Daddy, tell me about you. Lift me u-u-up." He will grow up to be just like his dad, doing for others and filled with u-u-understanding.

Personality trait: Utterly Unselfish
Favorite food: Umbrella fruit and upside-down cake

U is a vowel. Vowels are the letters that stick words together.

Trace me with your finger!
Draw me in the air.
Make me with clay.

All vowels are multicolored because they do lots of jobs and make more than one sound.

Bud is a mutt.*

> Kid, tap and blend the letters that are characters and read the words that are in black (high frequency words) without tapping and blending. Never use pictures to "read." Look at the pictures on the next page ONLY to confirm that you understood the words. I say yuck when you don't use us to read the words <u>WE</u> letters build.

*Mutt is an irregular spelling. Usually only the f, l, s and sometimes z are doubled at the end of a single syllable word. Mutt has two ts because of the word origin.

Bud is a mutt.

He is fun.

Close your eyes and make a picture in your mind with the words you just read. Turn the page and see what the author/illustrator imagined. Do they match what you thought the words said? Draw your own interpretation below the picture on the page. Everyone's pictures are a little different. That is part of the magic of reading.

Bud is a mutt.

Can you find the tiny vowels (u) in the illustration? Draw your illustration in the box below.

He is fun.

Can you find the tiny vowels (u) in the illustration? Draw your illustration in the box below.

Bud is a mutt.

He is fun.

Bud runs in the sun.

Bud is a mutt.

He is fun.

Bud runs in the sun.

Bud the pup runs in the mud.

Bud runs in the sun.

Can you find the tiny vowels (u) in the illustration? Draw your illustration in the box below.

Bud the pup runs in the mud.

Can you find the tiny vowels (u) in the illustration? Draw your illustration in the box below.

Bud is a mutt.

He is fun.

Bud runs in the sun.

Bud the pup runs in the mud.

Bud goes into the tub.

Bud is a mutt.

He is fun.

Bud runs in the sun.

Bud the pup runs in the mud.

Bud goes into the tub.

Bud gets a rub and a hug.

Bud goes into the tub.

Can you find the tiny vowels (u) in the illustration? Draw your illustration in the box below.

Bud gets a rub and a hug.

Can you find the tiny vowels (u) in the illustration? Draw your illustration in the box below.

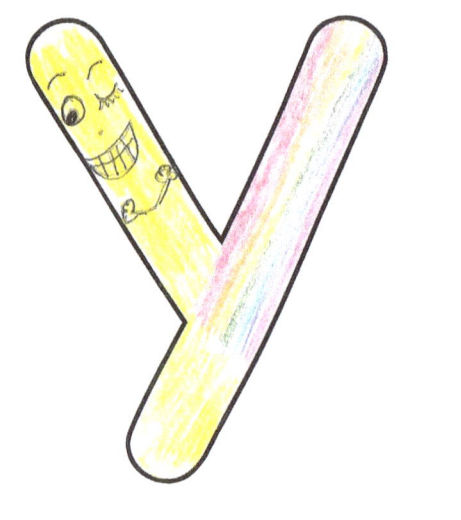

LETTER "Y" REVIEW

Y can be a consonant or a vowel.
He is a two-sound guy.

Y is the most curious and versatile letter of all. He is always asking questions and ready to help his friends. He is unique because he can be either a vowel or a consonant. Why not Y?

He says (insert three sounds here: Y as in yellow, I as in by, and E as in very). "Why? Why do you need to stick to being either a vowel or a consonant when you can be both? Why? Why? Why? Y? Y? Y? I have special powers of discovery. I can figure things out. I usually say y-y-yes. I sometimes take over for i when i is too busy thinking about himself as in the words by and my. Why? I even sometimes help e. Yes, I am very fine."

Little baby y says, "Looky, looky, Daddy! I can make so many sounds and help the other letters just like you. My favorite color is y-y-yellow."

Personality trait: He is a yes-man!
Favorite food: Yellow squash and my candy!

Y is sometimes a vowel.
Vowels are the letters that stick words together.

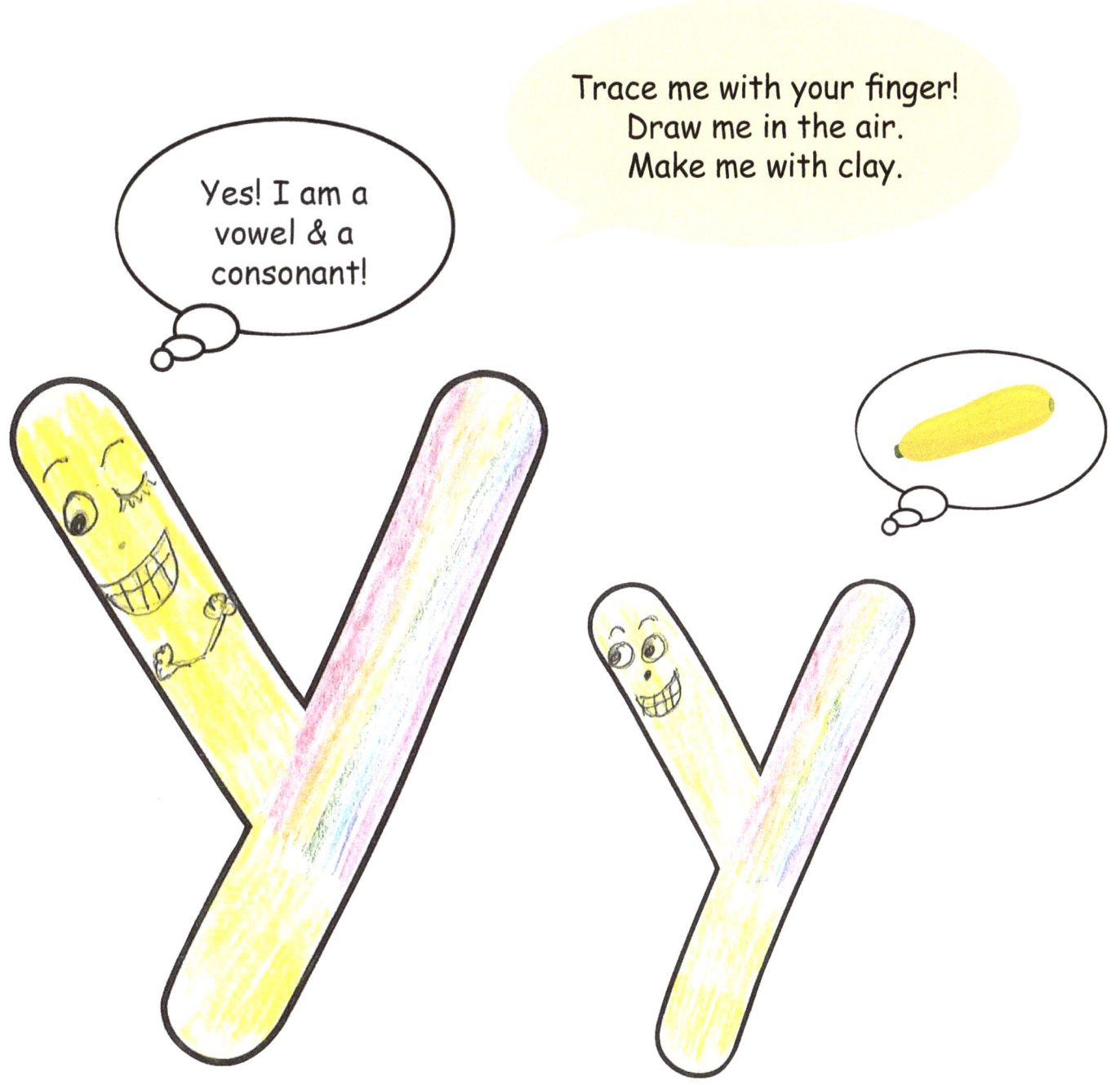

The sound we make depends on where we sit in a word, for example, yellow, by, or daddy.

Yes! At the beginning of a word y is a consonant. If he sits anywhere else he says ī or ē.

Sky can fly!

> Kid, tap and blend the letters that are characters and read the words that are in black (high frequency words) without tapping and blending. Never use pictures to "read." Look at the pictures on the next page ONLY to confirm that you understood the words. I get so surprised when you don't use us to read the words WE letters build.

*Note in vowel pairs y says a different sound than long i's sound. These are ay (long a), ey (long e) and oy (oi as in boy).

Sky can fly!

Sky is shy.

Close your eyes and make a picture in your mind with the words you just read. Turn the page and see what the author/illustrator imagined. Do they match what you thought the words said? Draw your own interpretation below the picture on the page. Everyone's pictures are a little different. That is part of the magic of reading.

Sky can fly!

Can you find the tiny vowels (y) in the illustration? Draw your illustration in the box below.

Draw your illustration in the box below. Can you find the tiny vowels (y) in the illustration?

Sky can fly!

Sky is shy.

By* Sky is a fly.

*By here means in proximity to or near.

Sky can fly!

Sky is shy.

By Sky is a fly.

"Ty the fly is my fly," says Sky.

By Sky is a fly.

Can you find the tiny vowels (y) in the illustration? Draw your illustration in the box below.

"Ty the fly is my fly," says Sky.

Can you find the tiny vowels (y) in the illustration? Draw your illustration in the box below.

Sky can fly!

Sky is shy.

By Sky is a fly.

"Ty the fly is my fly," says Sky.

"Fly, Sky, fly," says Ty to Sky.

Sky can fly!

Sky is shy.

By Sky is a fly.

"Ty the fly is my fly," says Sky.

"Fly, Sky, fly," says Ty to Sky.

"I will try," says Sky. Oh my, by and by, Sky does fly.

"Fly Sky, fly," says Ty to Sky.

Can you find the tiny vowels (y) in the illustration? Draw your illustration in the box below.

"I will try," says Sky.
Oh my, by and by, Sky does fly.

Can you find the tiny vowels (y) in the illustration? Draw your illustration in the box below.

Vowel Review

Vowels are the letters that stick words together. Every word and each syllable needs a vowel. They are difficult to master and require a lot of practice.

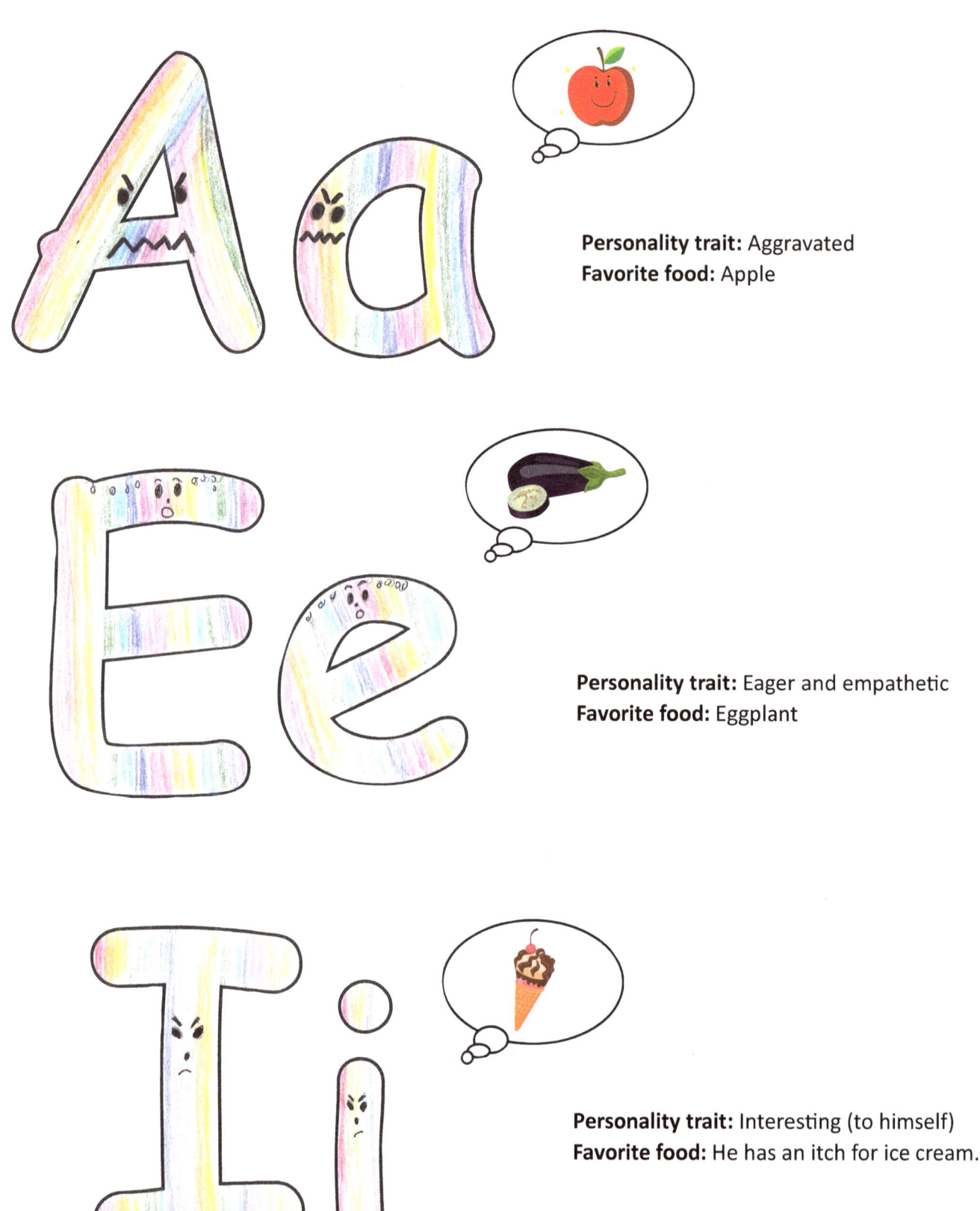

Personality trait: Aggravated
Favorite food: Apple

Personality trait: Eager and empathetic
Favorite food: Eggplant

Personality trait: Interesting (to himself)
Favorite food: He has an itch for ice cream.

Personality trait: Open
Favorite food: Oatmeal for breakfast and octopus on special occasions.

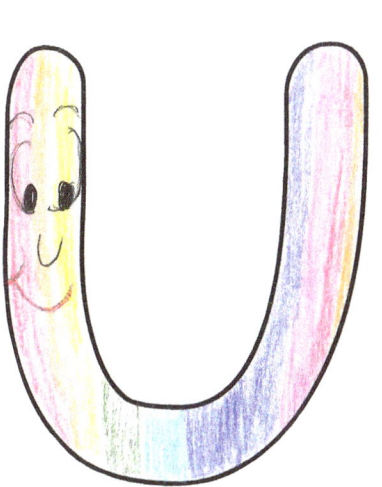

Personality trait: Unselfish
Favorite foods: Umbrella fruit and upside-down cake

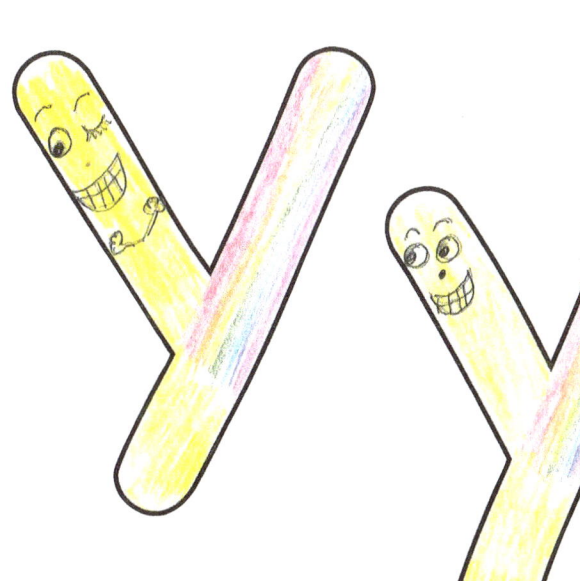

Personality trait: He is a yes-man!
Favorite food: Yellow squash

The cat met Ben,
Jen the red hen,
Jim the pig,
Mom Frog,
Ty and Sky.

The cat met Ben,
Jen the red hen,
Jim the pig,
Mom Frog,
Ty and Sky.

"I am not a sad cat now, I am a glad cat!"

The cat met Ben, Jen the red hen, Jim the pig, Mom Frog, Ty and Sky.

Draw your illustration in the box below.

"I am not a sad cat now, I am a glad cat!"

Draw your illustration in the box below.

The cat met Ben,
Jen the red hen,
Jim the pig,
Mom Frog,
Ty and Sky.

"I am not a sad cat now,
I am a glad cat!"

"Let's do a jig?" said Jim
the fit pig to the glad cat.

The cat met Ben,
Jen the red hen,
Jim the pig,
Mom Frog,
Ty and Sky.

"I am not a sad cat now,
I am a glad cat!"

"Let's do a jig?" said Jim the fit pig to the glad cat.

"Yes!" they all said. They did jig and jag and hop and bop. It was fun.

"Let's do a jig?" said Jim the fit pig to the glad cat.

Draw your illustration in the box below.

"Yes!" they all said. They did jig and jag and hop and bop. It was fun.

Draw your illustration in the box below.

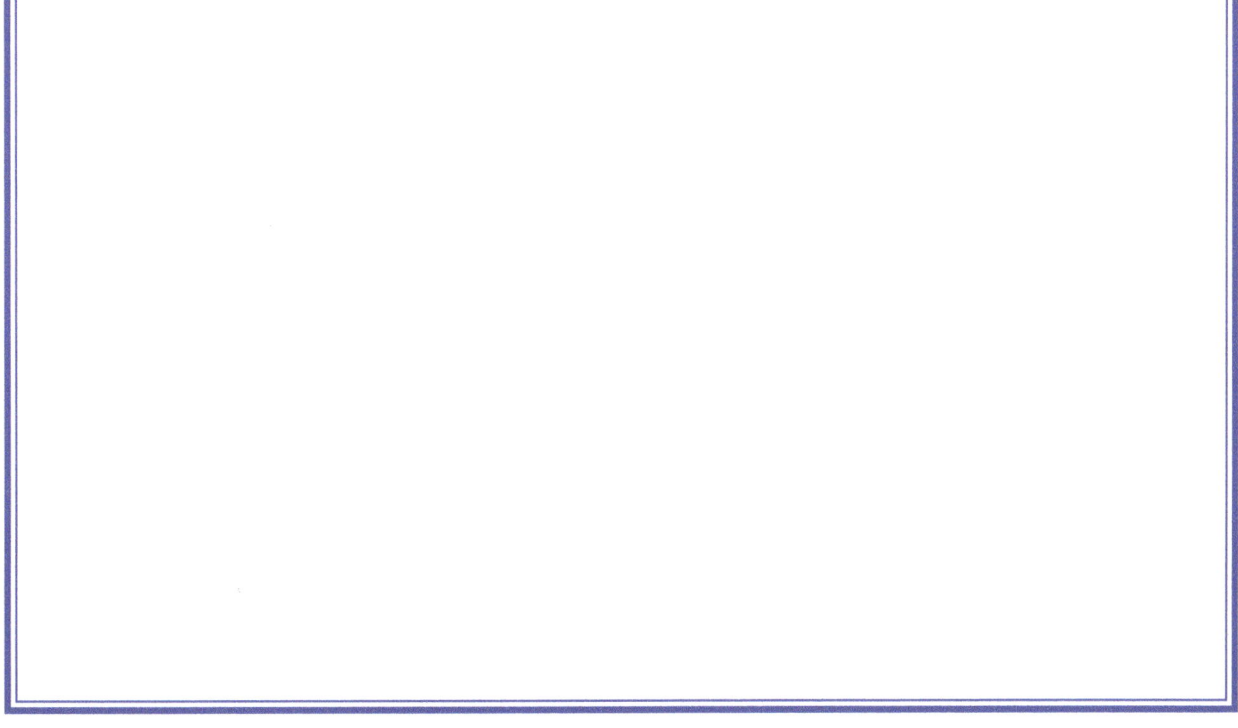

The cat met Ben, Jen the red hen, Jim the pig, Mom Frog, Ty and Sky.

"I am not a sad cat now, I am a glad cat!"

"Let's do a jig?" said Jim the fit pig to the glad cat.

"Yes!" they all said. They did jig and jag and hop and bop. It was fun.

It was lots of fun for Jim the fit pig and the glad cat.

The cat met Ben, Jen the red hen, Jim the pig, Mom Frog, Ty and Sky.

"I am not a sad cat now, I am a glad cat!"

"Let's do a jig?" said Jim the fit pig to the glad cat.

"Yes!" they all said. They did jig and jag and hop and bop. It was fun.

It was lots of fun for Jim the fit pig and the glad cat.

It was not fun for Pat the rat. "Nuts," he said.

It was lots of fun for Jim the fit pig and the glad cat.

Draw your illustration in the box below.

It was not fun for Pat the rat. "Nuts," he said.

Draw your illustration in the box below.

103

HIGH FREQUENCY WORDS

Sight words or high frequency words make up about 75 percent of beginning books for children. These words sometimes do not follow typical letter pattern/phonics rules although many do. We want our children to recognize these words automatically so that they don't run out of cognitive fuel decoding all of the words on the page. Included here, are the first group for your child to learn. Once they know these and their letter sounds, they will be ready to start reading decodable books!

To teach these words, first say the word while using your pointer and middle finger of the hand that you write with to trace a line in the direction of the arrow under the word. Next have your child do the same. Repeat this see-and-say exercise.

Next try spell reading. Do the previous exercise and add this step... Ask your little reader to spell the word after they say it. For example, have them say "the" as they underline the word with their finger. Next have them spell "t-h-e" as they underline the word with their finger and after they spell it have them say it again (the, t-h-e, the).

Have your child skywrite the word.

You can also have them sing sight words - first singing the sight word, then singing/spelling it, then singing/saying it.

Have your child color these sight words.

Review the words and check the boxes below them to indicate when your child has read the word ten times without hesitation. Then you can call that word a graduate!

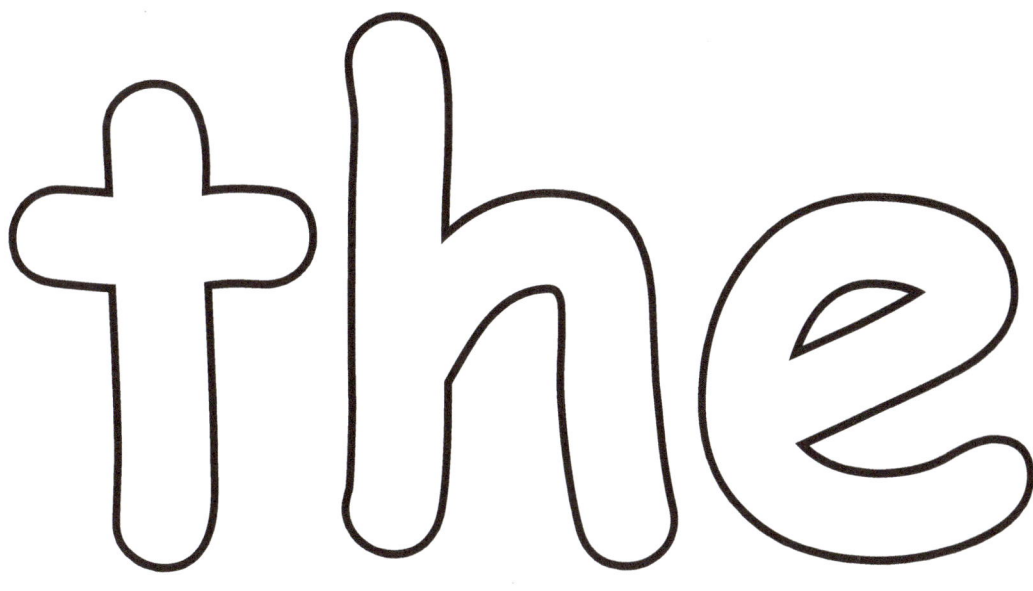

Check the boxes below each time the word is read without hesitation.

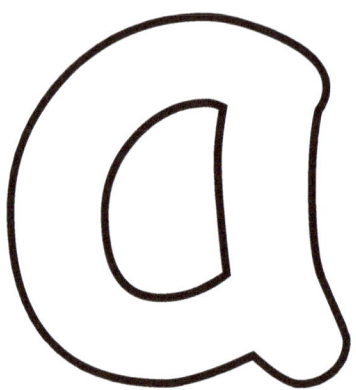

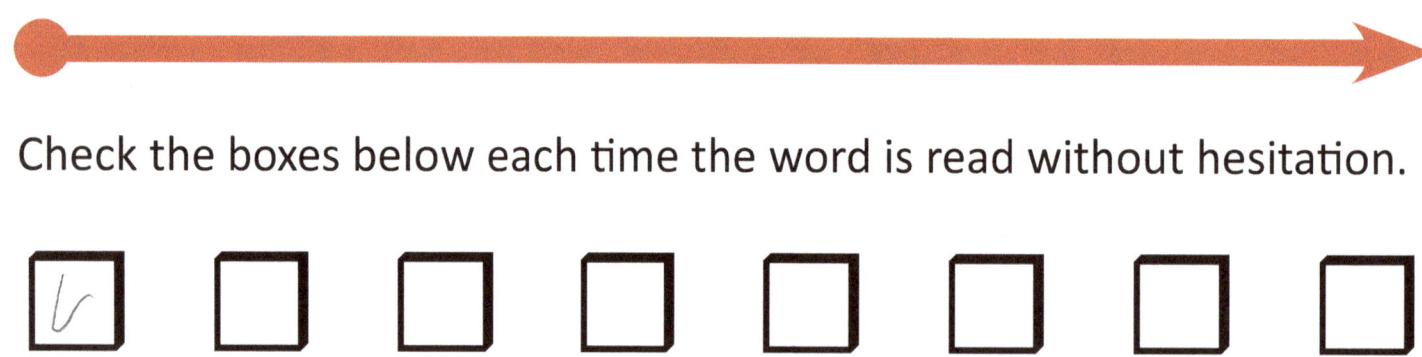

Check the boxes below each time the word is read without hesitation.

Check the boxes below each time the word is read without hesitation.

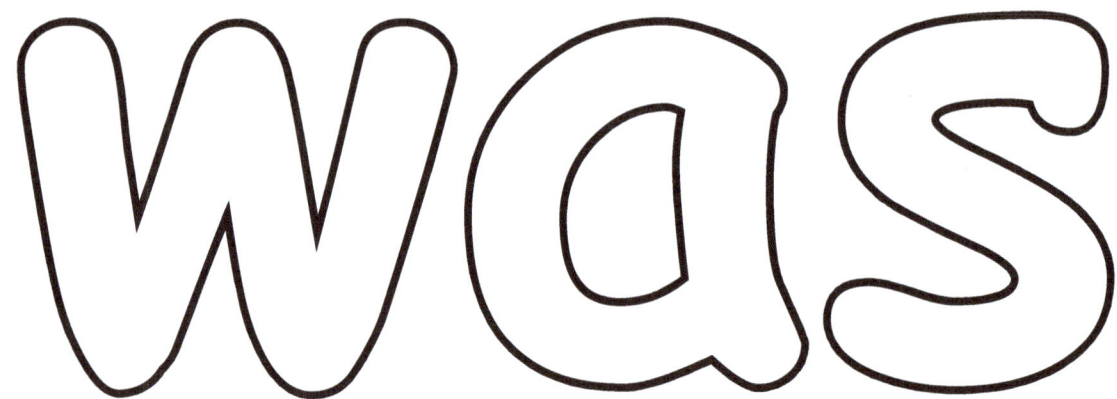

Check the boxes below each time the word is read without hesitation.

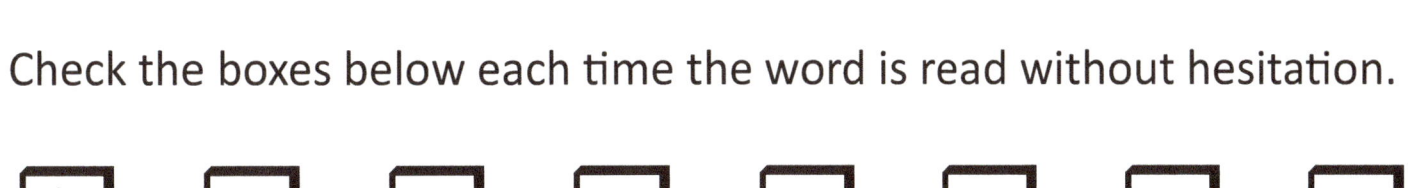

Check the boxes below each time the word is read without hesitation.

Check the boxes below each time the word is read without hesitation.

Check the boxes below each time the word is read without hesitation.

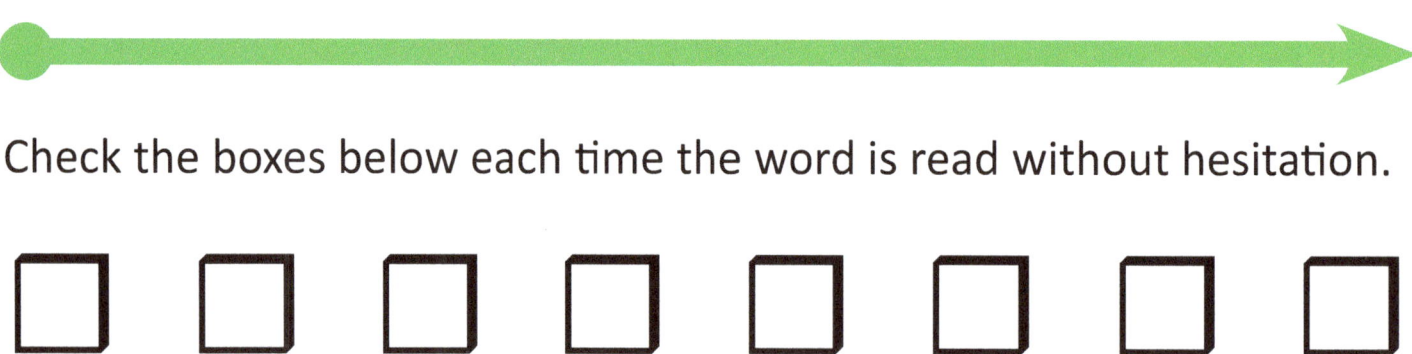

Check the boxes below each time the word is read without hesitation.

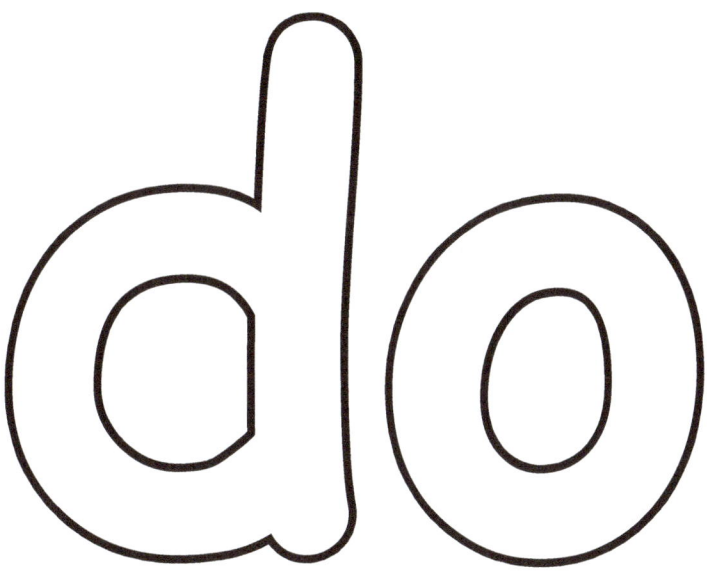

Check the boxes below each time the word is read without hesitation.

☐ ☐ ☐ ☐ ☐ ☐ ☐ ☐

Check the boxes below each time the word is read without hesitation.

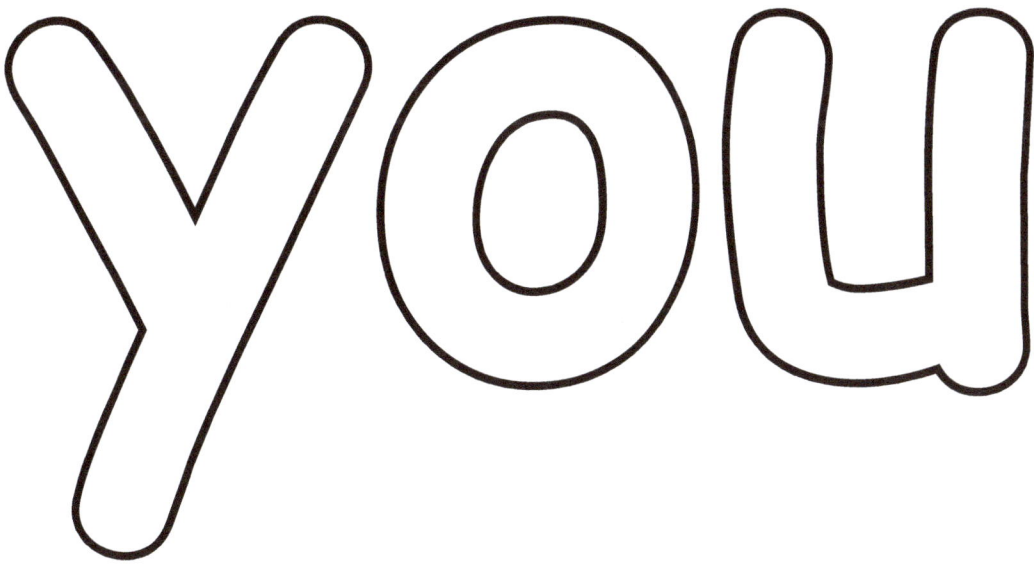

Check the boxes below each time the word is read without hesitation.

Check the boxes below each time the word is read without hesitation.

Check the boxes below each time the word is read without hesitation.

  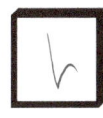     

Check the boxes below each time the word is read without hesitation.

Check the boxes below each time the word is read without hesitation.

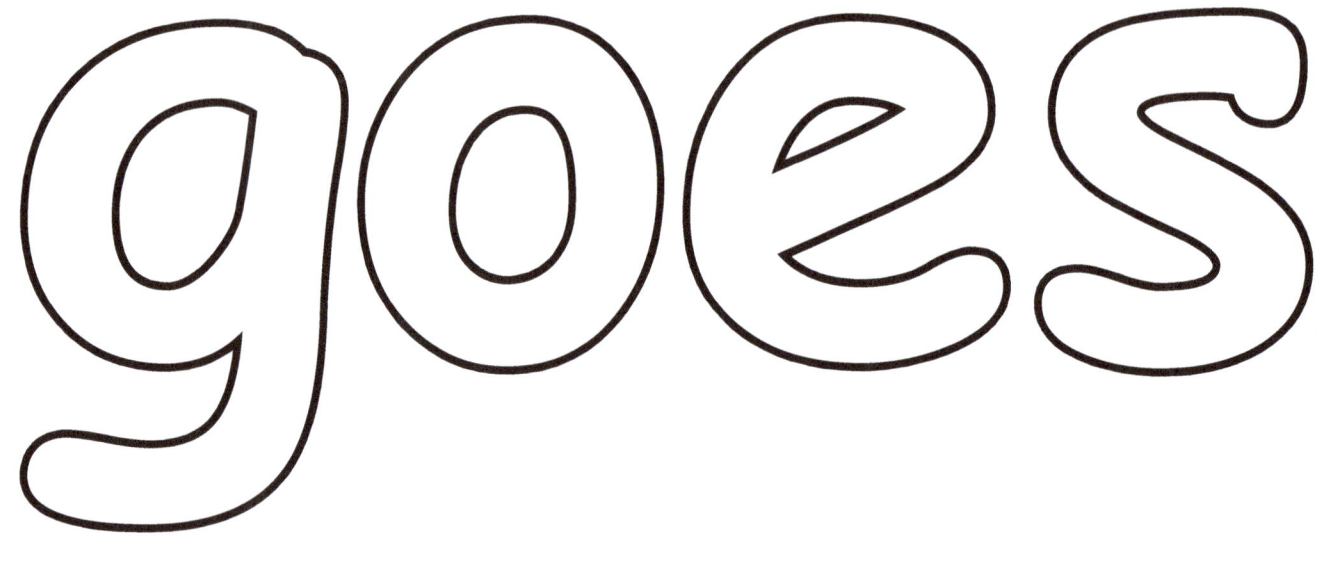

Check the boxes below each time the word is read without hesitation.

☐ ☐ ☐ ☐ ☐ ☐ ☐ ☐

Check the boxes below each time the word is read without hesitation.

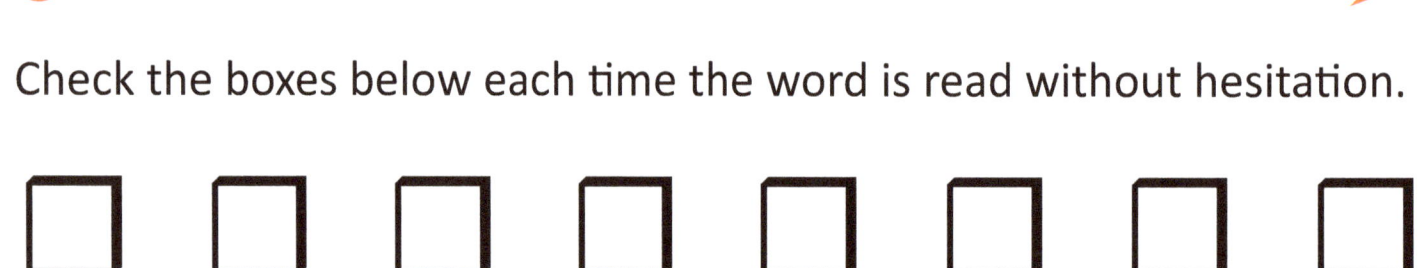

Check the boxes below each time the word is read without hesitation.

☐ ☐ ☐ ☐ ☐ ☐ ☐ ☐

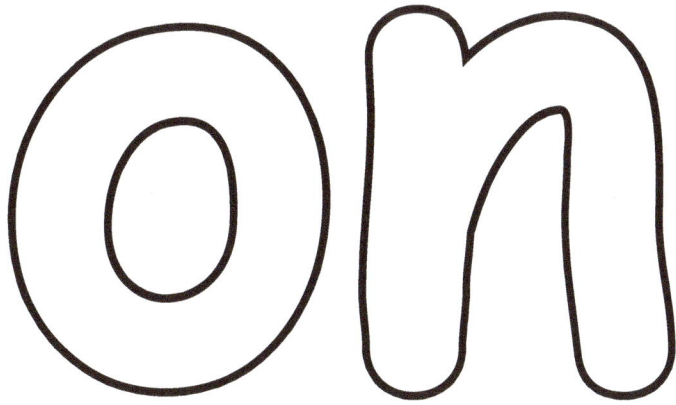

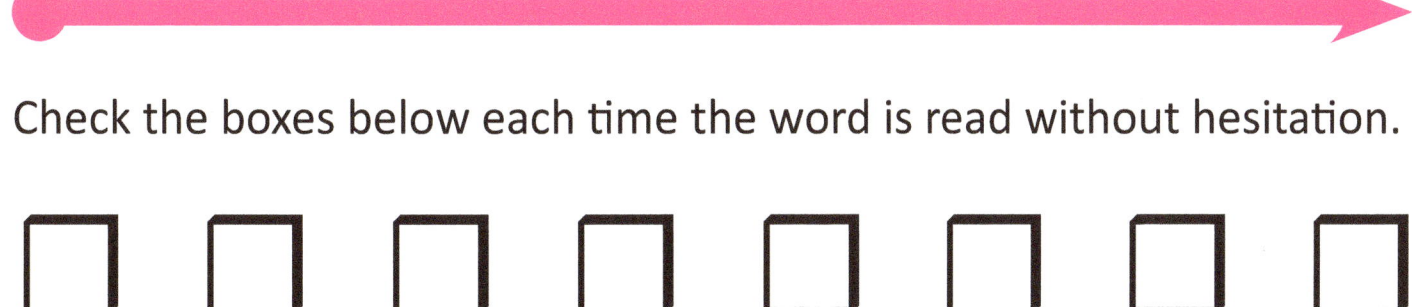

Check the boxes below each time the word is read without hesitation.

☐ ☐ ☐ ☐ ☐ ☐ ☐ ☐

Check the boxes below each time the word is read without hesitation.

☐ ☐ ☐ ☐ ☐ ☐ ☐ ☐

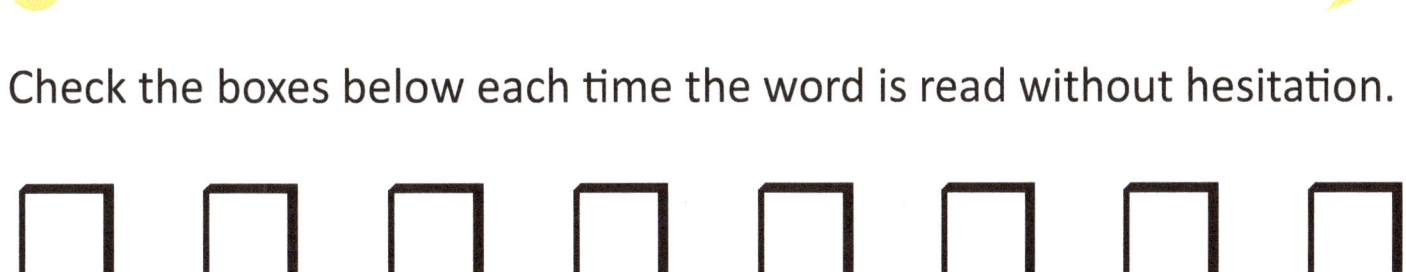

Check the boxes below each time the word is read without hesitation.

☐ ☐ ☐ ☐ ☐ ☐ ☐ ☐

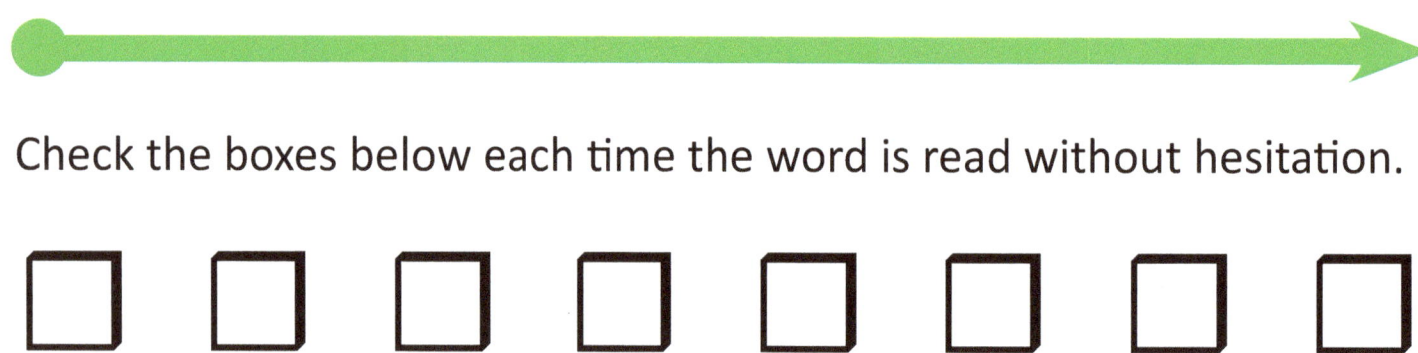

Check the boxes below each time the word is read without hesitation.

☐ ☐ ☐ ☐ ☐ ☐ ☐ ☐

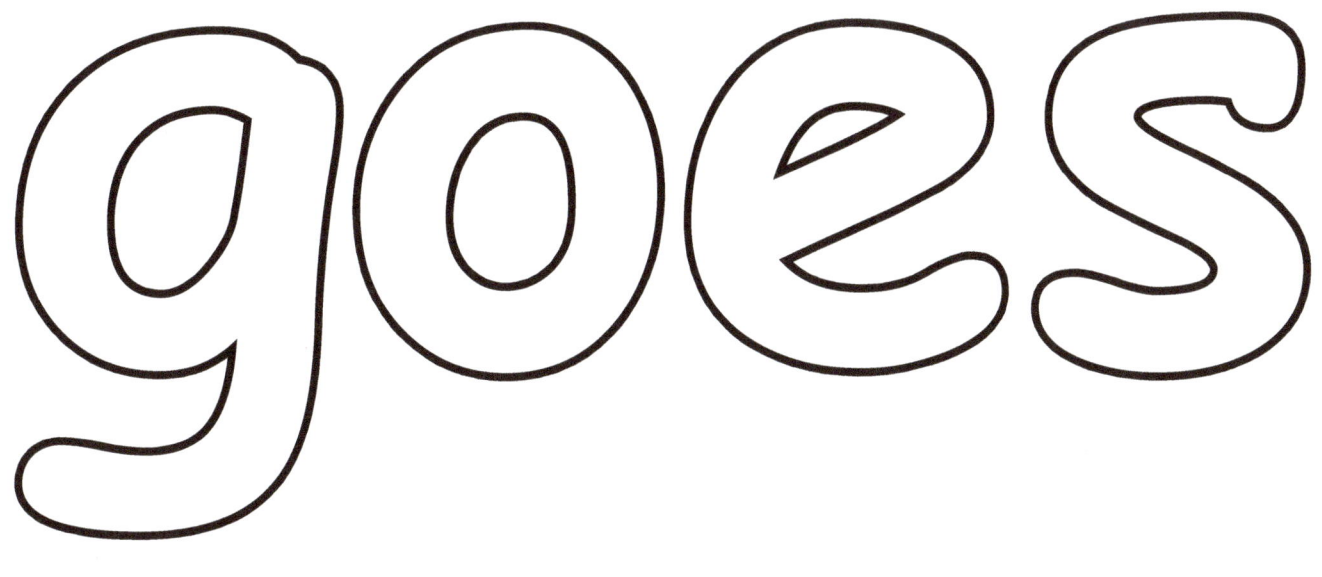

Check the boxes below each time the word is read without hesitation.

☐ ☐ ☐ ☐ ☐ ☐ ☐ ☐

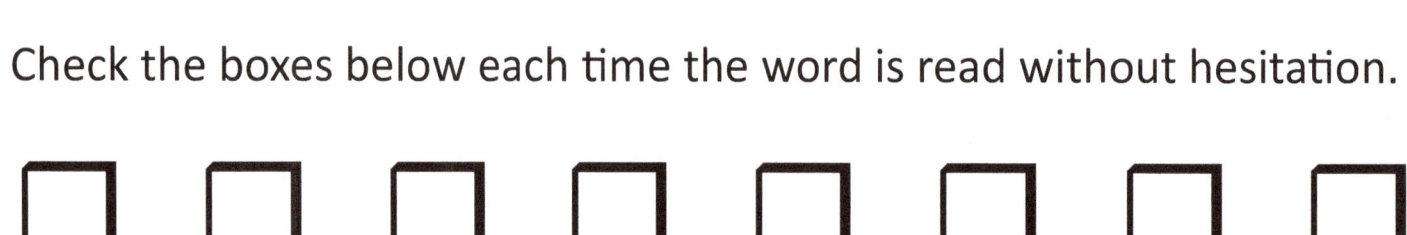

Check the boxes below each time the word is read without hesitation.

☐ ☐ ☐ ☐ ☐ ☐ ☐ ☐

Check the boxes below each time the word is read without hesitation.

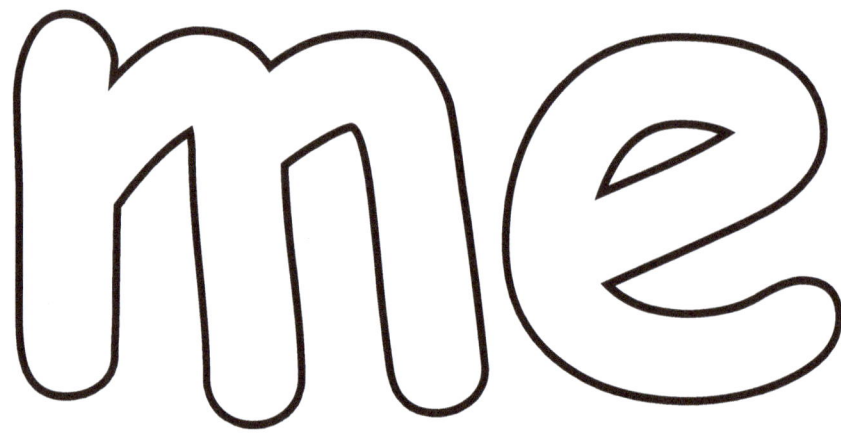

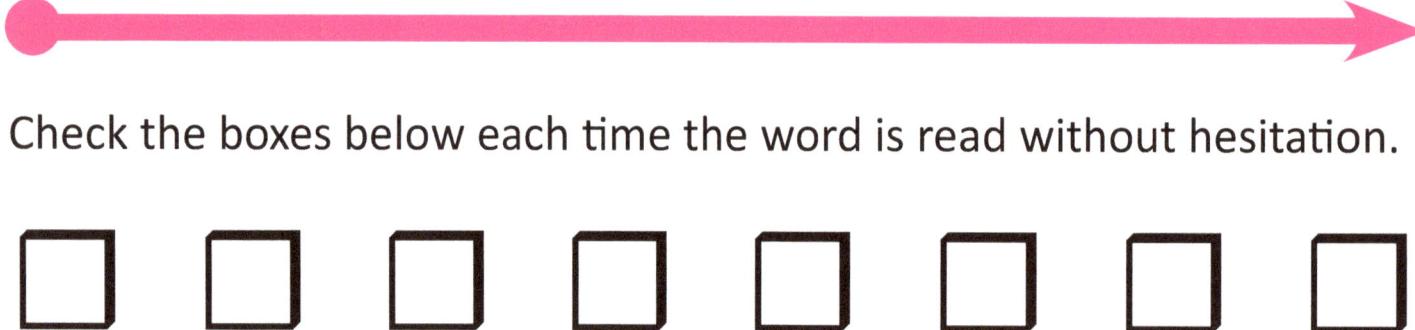

Check the boxes below each time the word is read without hesitation.

☐ ☐ ☐ ☐ ☐ ☐ ☐ ☐

Check the boxes below each time the word is read without hesitation.

☐ ☐ ☐ ☐ ☐ ☐ ☐ ☐

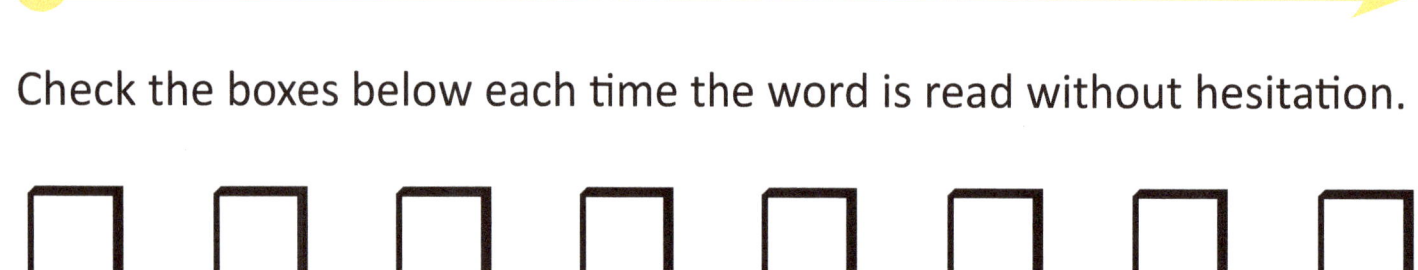

Check the boxes below each time the word is read without hesitation.

☐ ☐ ☐ ☐ ☐ ☐ ☐ ☐

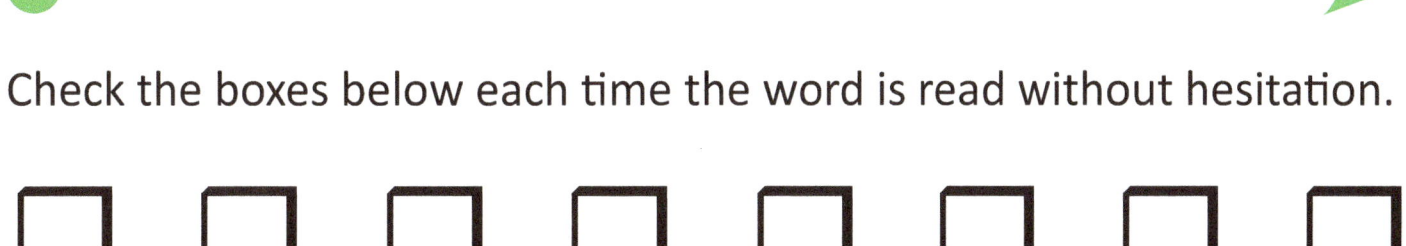

Check the boxes below each time the word is read without hesitation.

☐ ☐ ☐ ☐ ☐ ☐ ☐ ☐

Check the boxes below each time the word is read without hesitation.

Check the boxes below each time the word is read without hesitation.

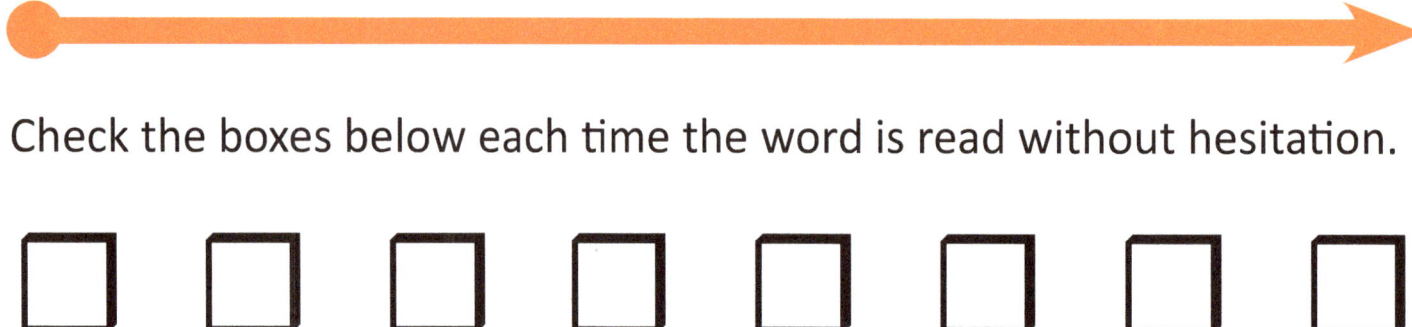

Check the boxes below each time the word is read without hesitation.

☐ ☐ ☐ ☐ ☐ ☐ ☐ ☐

they

Check the boxes below each time the word is read without hesitation.

☐ ☐ ☐ ☐ ☐ ☐ ☐ ☐

Check the boxes below each time the word is read without hesitation.

Check the boxes below each time the word is read without hesitation.